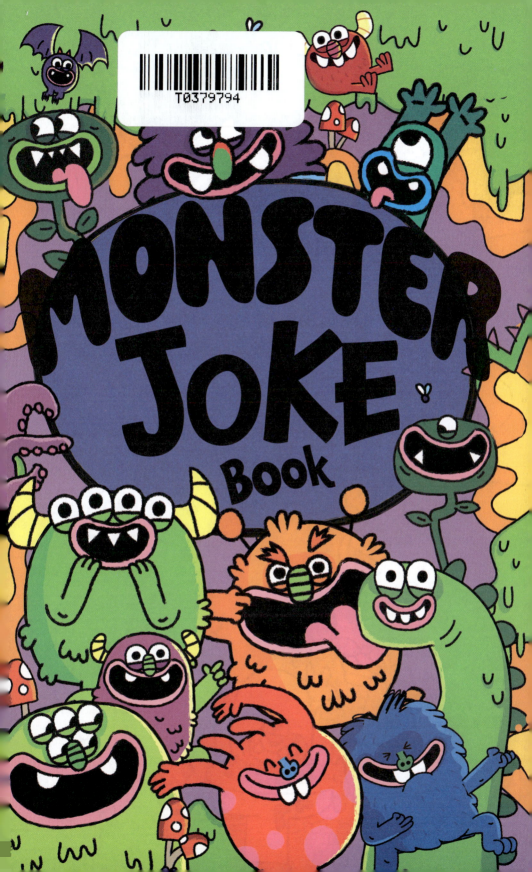

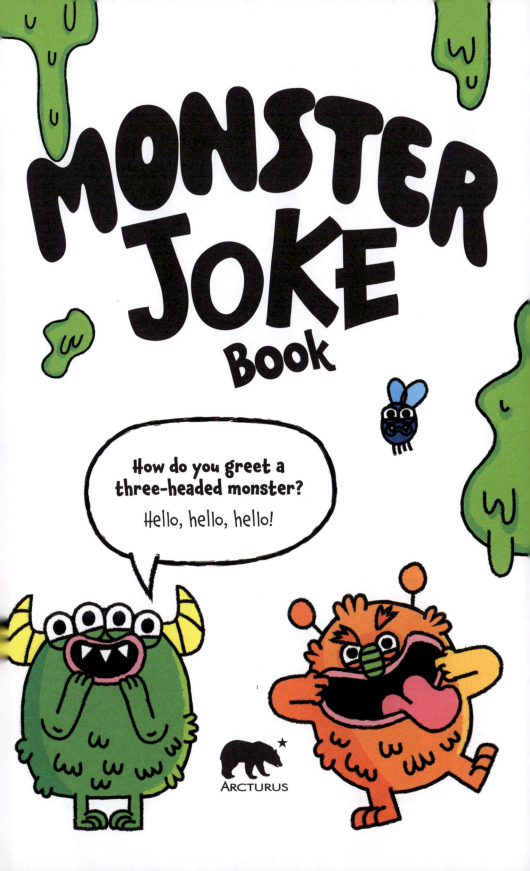

ARCTURUS

This edition published in 2025 by Arcturus Publishing Limited
26/27 Bickels Yard, 151–153 Bermondsey Street,
London SE1 3HA

Copyright © Arcturus Holdings Limited

All rights reserved. No part of this publication may be reproduced, stored in a retrieval system, or transmitted, in any form or by any means, electronic, mechanical, photocopying, recording, or otherwise, without prior written permission in accordance with the provisions of the Copyright Act 1956 (as amended). Any person or persons who do any unauthorized act in relation to this publication may be liable to criminal prosecution and civil claims for damages.

Author: Lisa Regan
Illustrator: Steven Wood
Designer: Nathan Balsom
Editor: Becca Clunes
Editorial Manager: Joe Harris
Design Manager: Rosie Bellwood-Moyler

ISBN: 978-1-3988-5637-0
CH012417NT
Supplier 29, Date 0625, PI 00010140

Printed in China

Contents

Chapter 1	Monster Mayhem	7
Chapter 2	Frightfully Funny	25
Chapter 3	Nice to Eat You!	41
Chapter 4	Ghastly Giggles	59
Chapter 5	Fang You Very Much	75
Chapter 6	Rib-Ticklers and Funny Bones	93
Chapter 7	Scare Tactics	109
Chapter 8	Exsqueeze Me!	127
Chapter 9	Hideous Hilarity	143
Chapter 10	Horrible Howlers	161

Chapter 1
Monster Mayhem

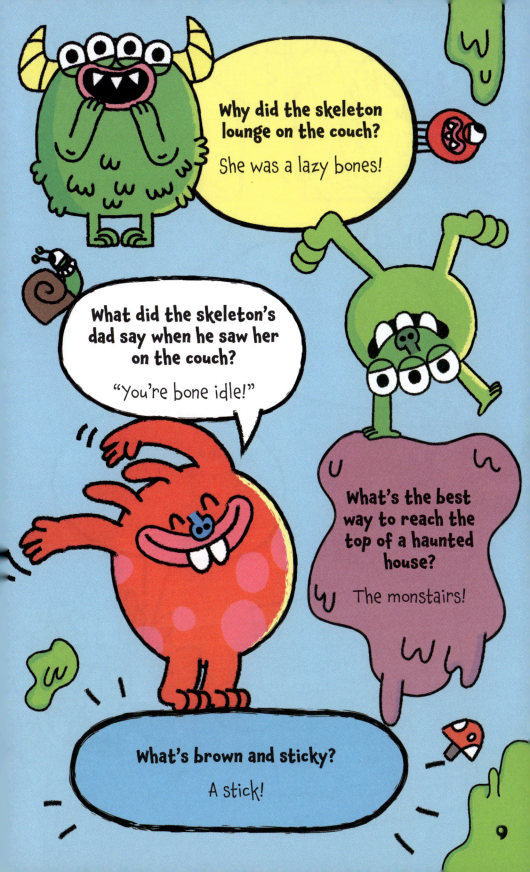

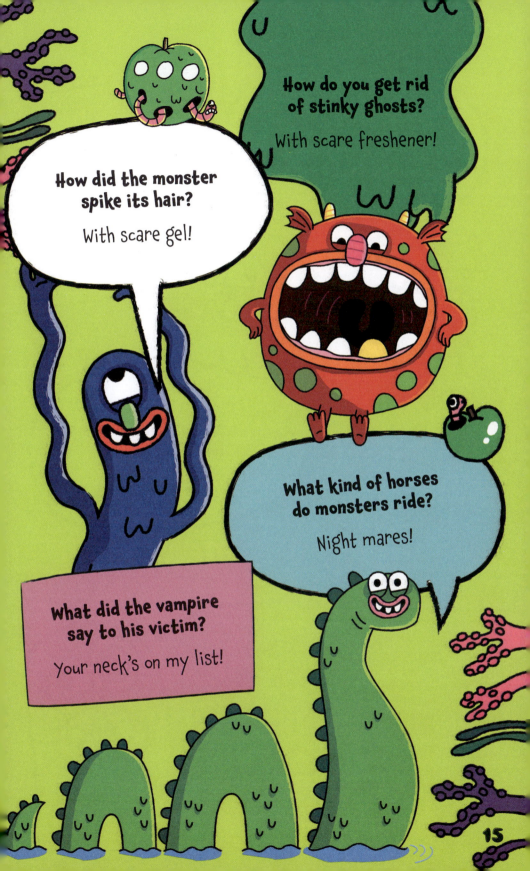

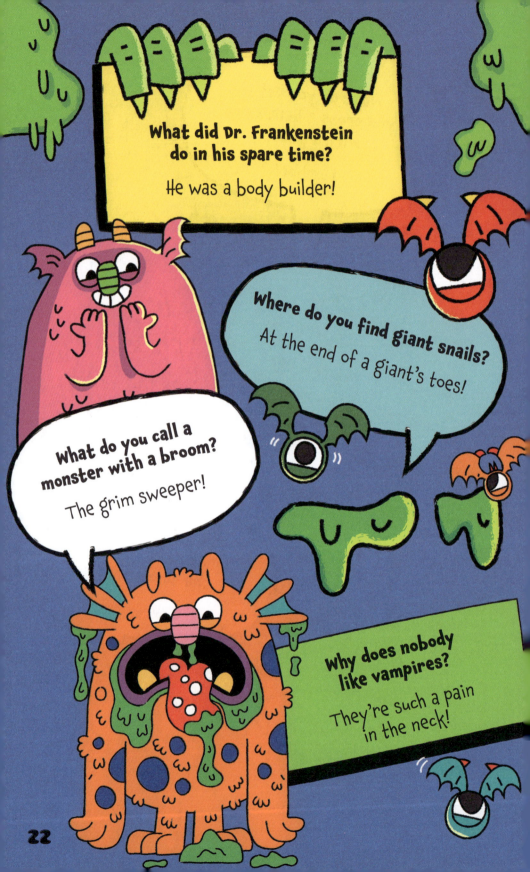

Chapter 2
Frightfully Funny

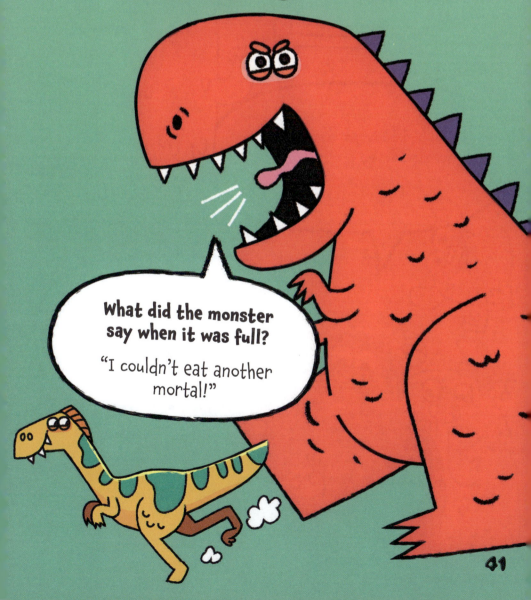
Chapter 3
Nice to Eat You!

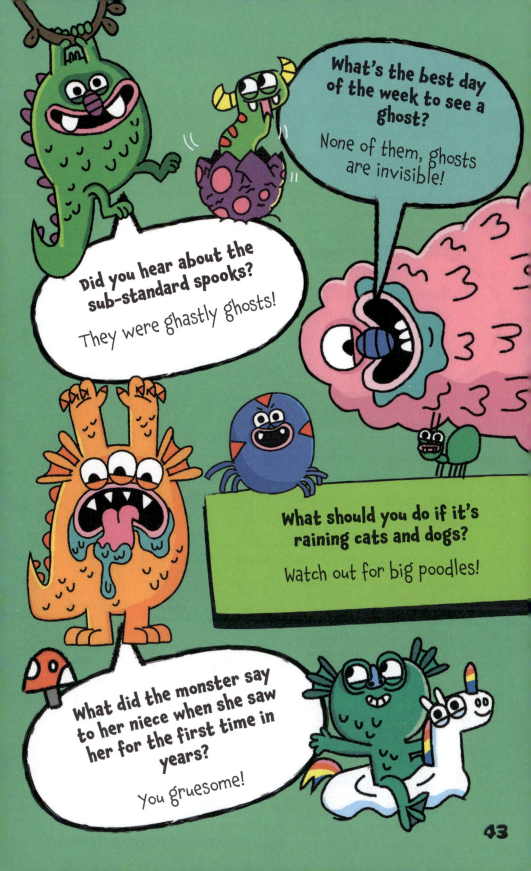

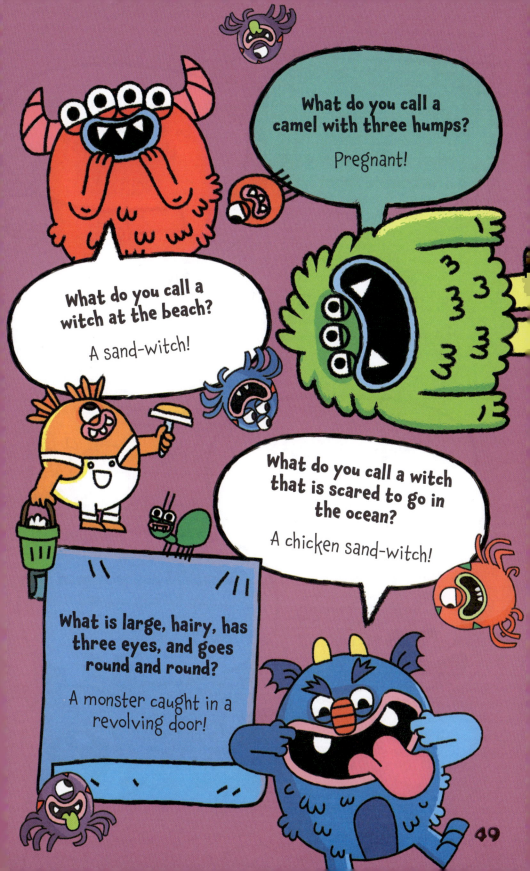

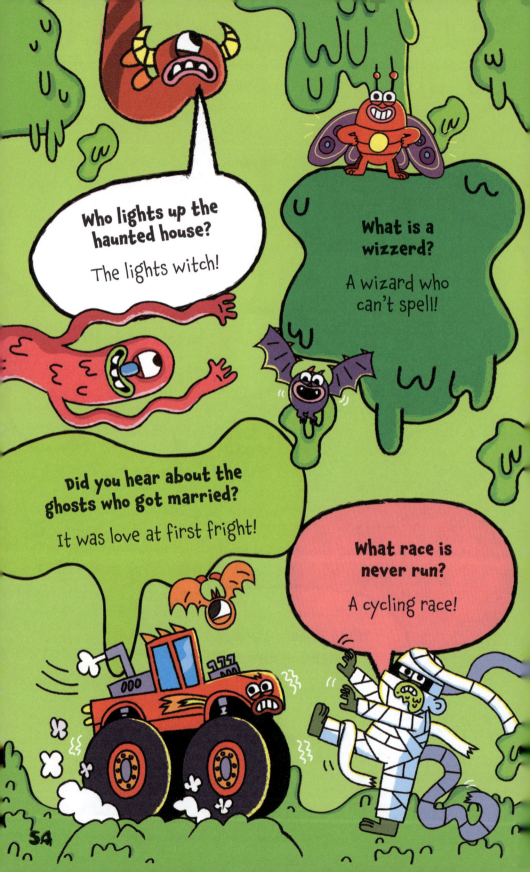

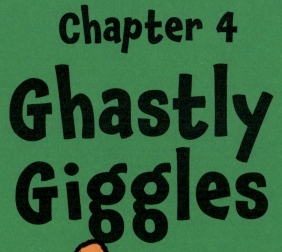

Chapter 4
Ghastly Giggles

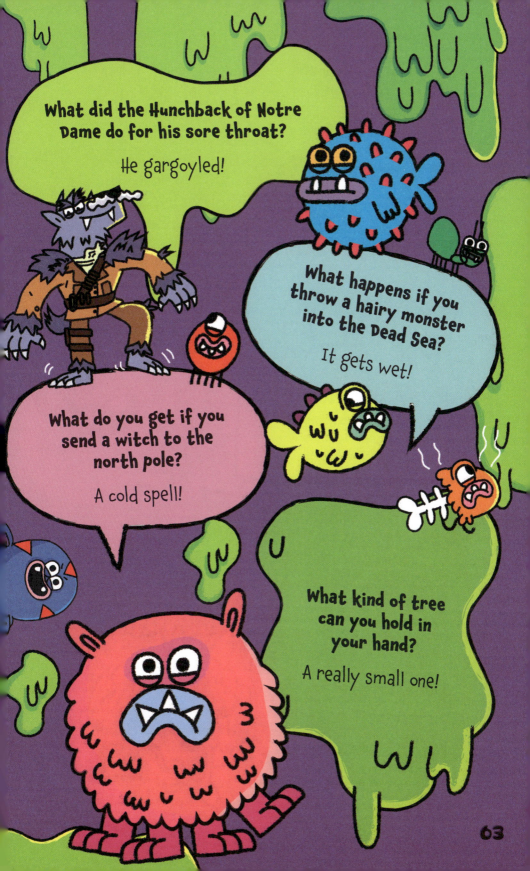

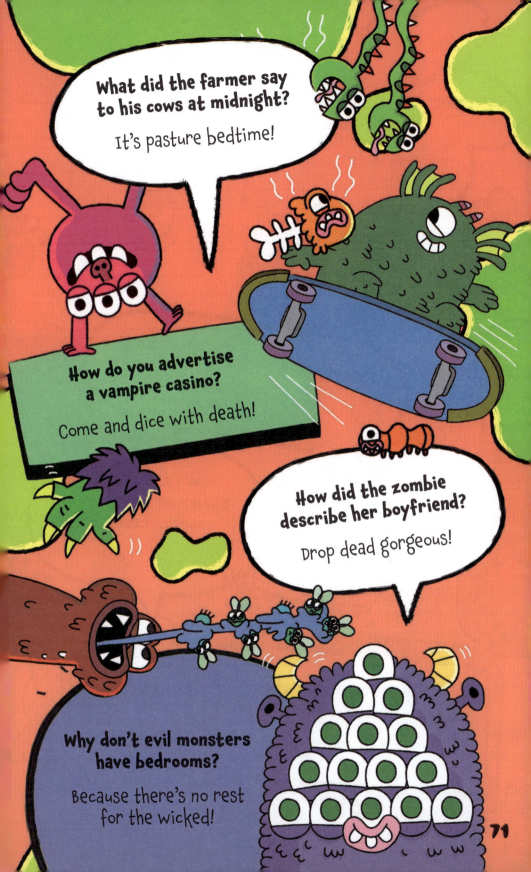

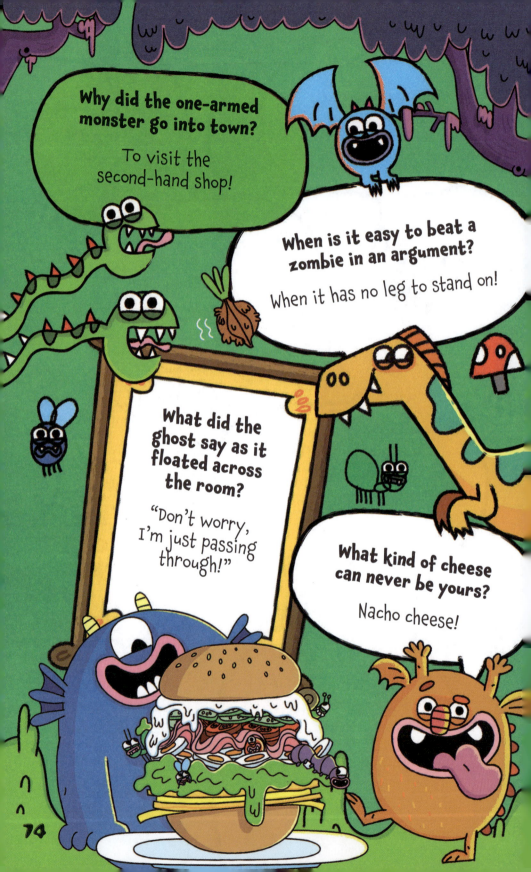

Chapter 5
Fang You Very Much

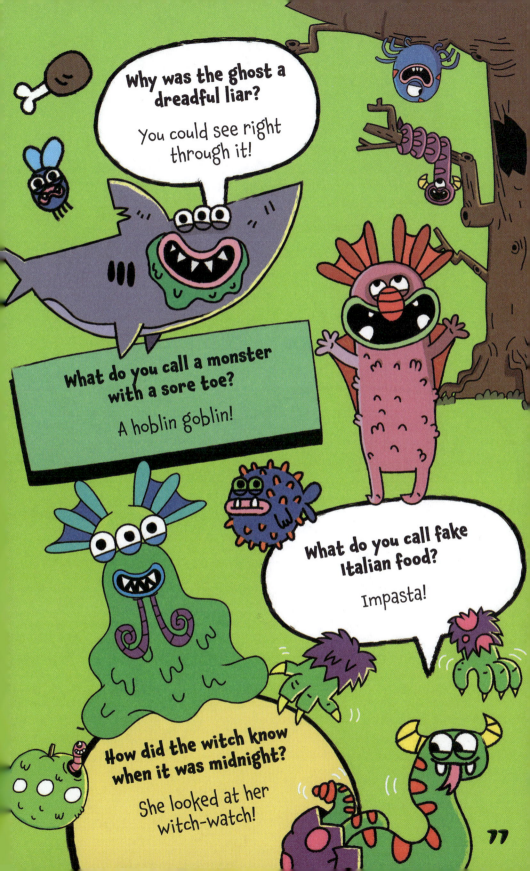

Chapter 6
Rib-Ticklers and Funny Bones

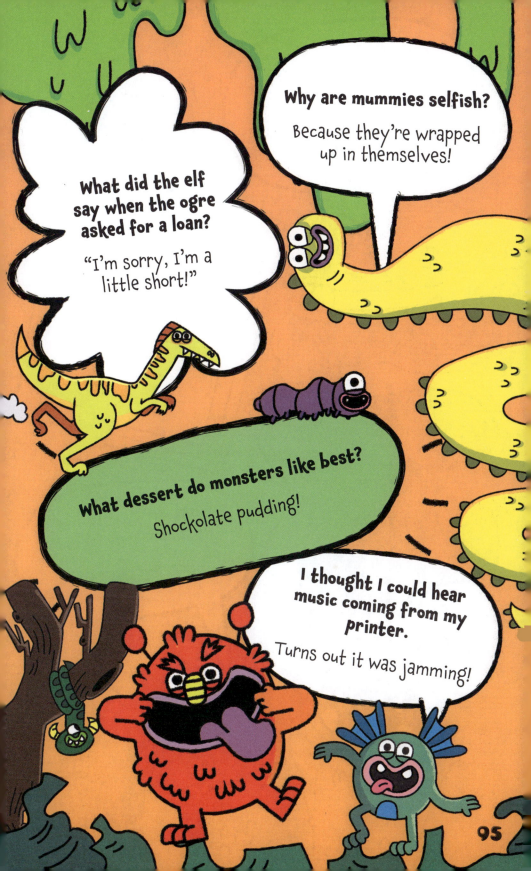

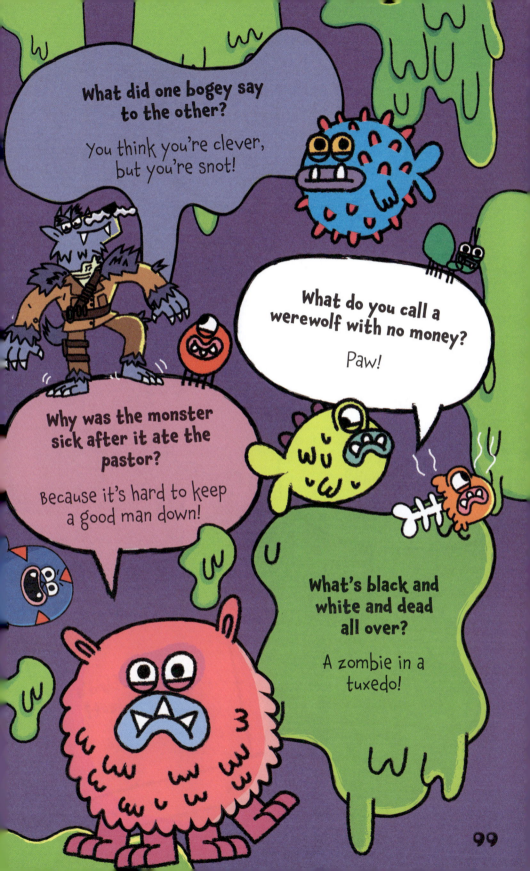

Chapter 7
Scare Tactics

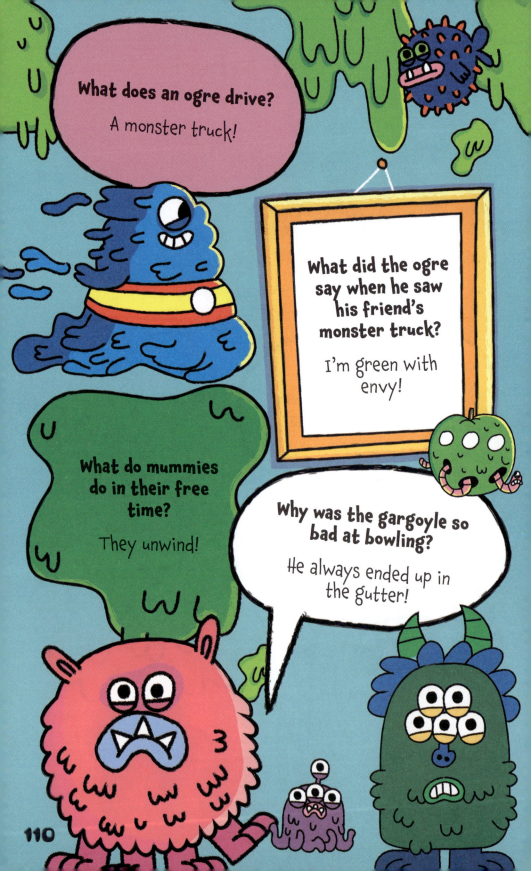

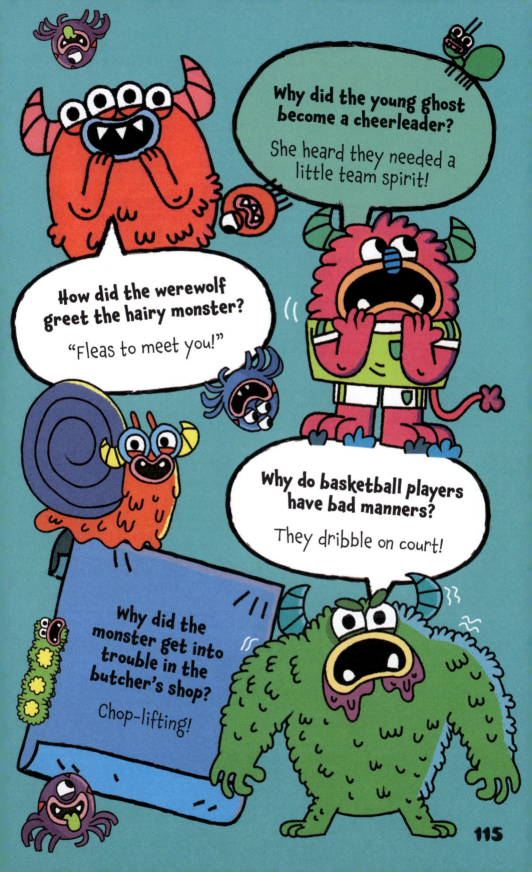

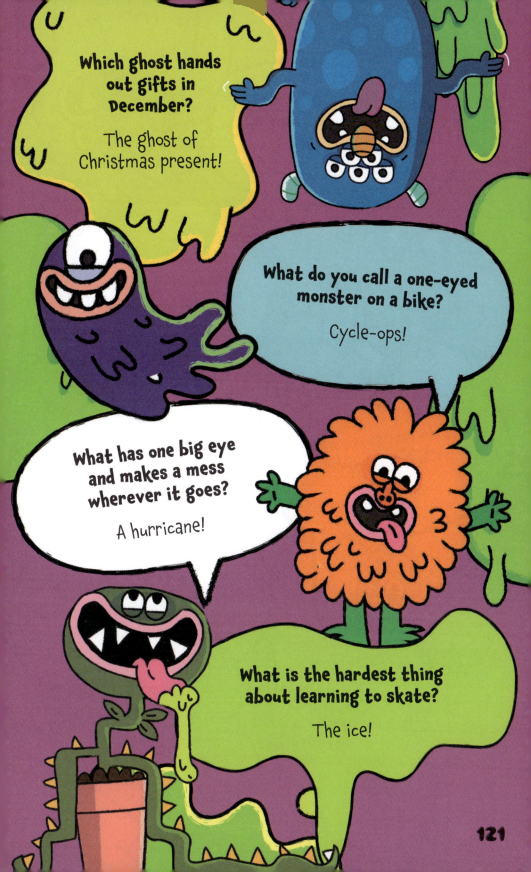

Chapter 8
Exsqueeze Me!

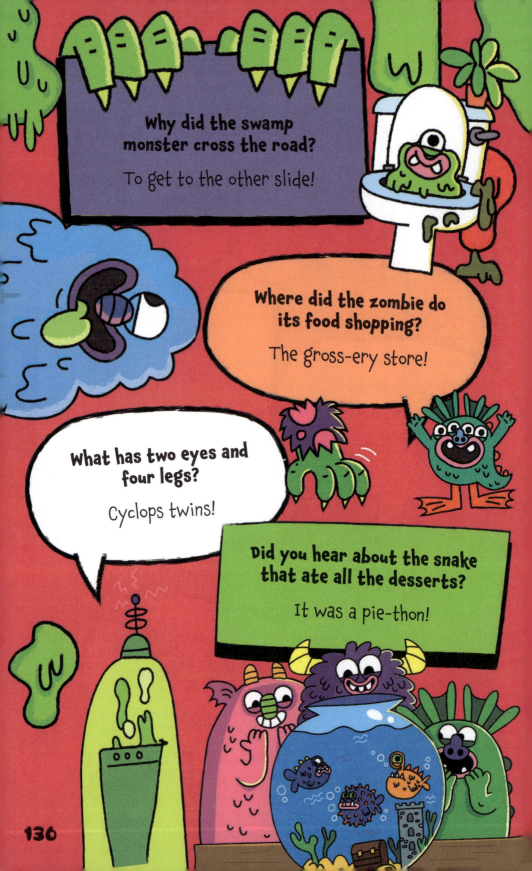

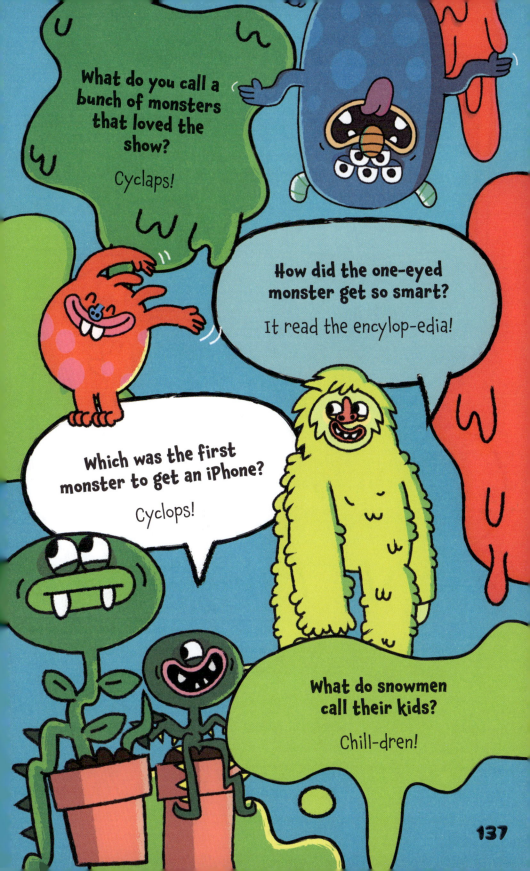

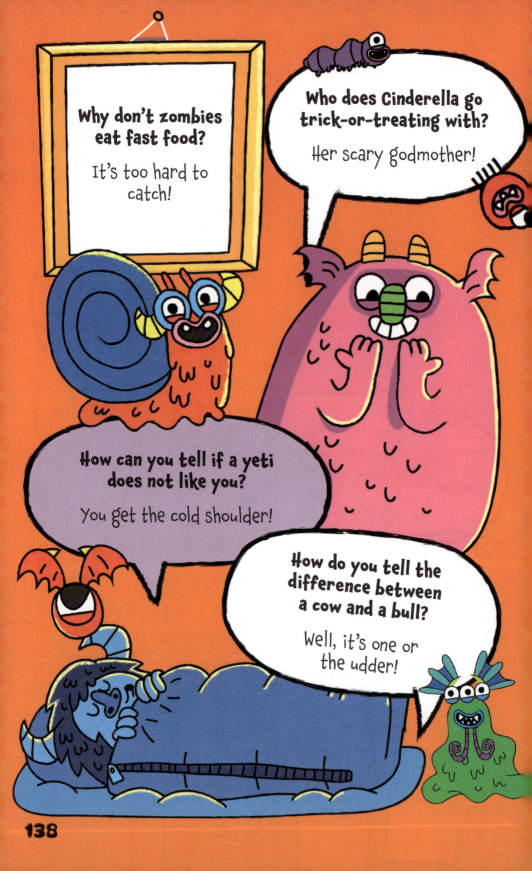

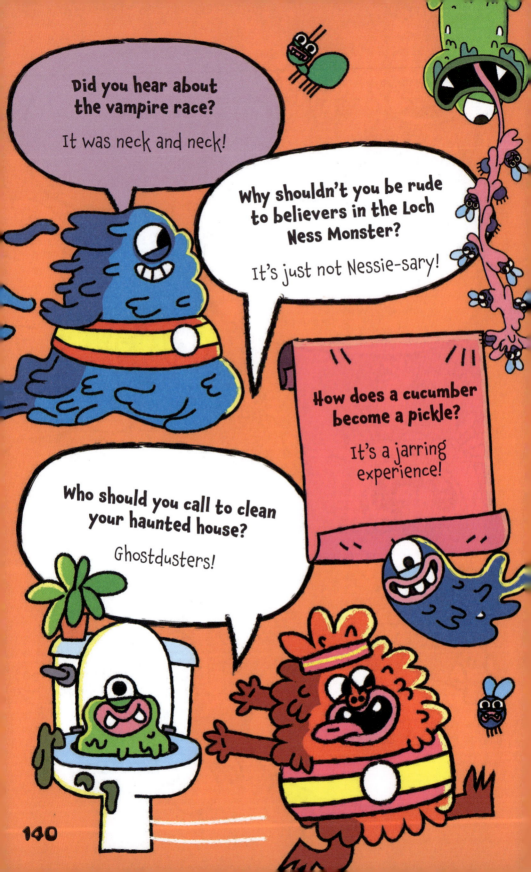

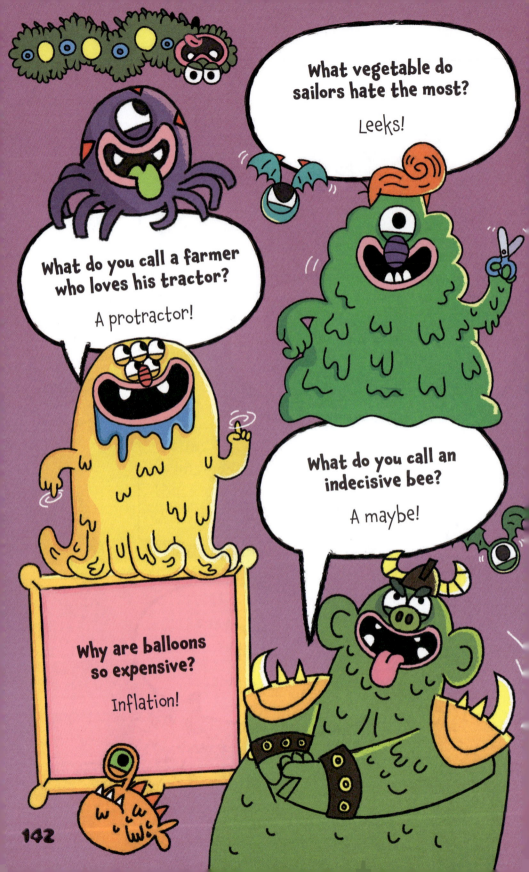

Chapter 9
Hideous Hilarity

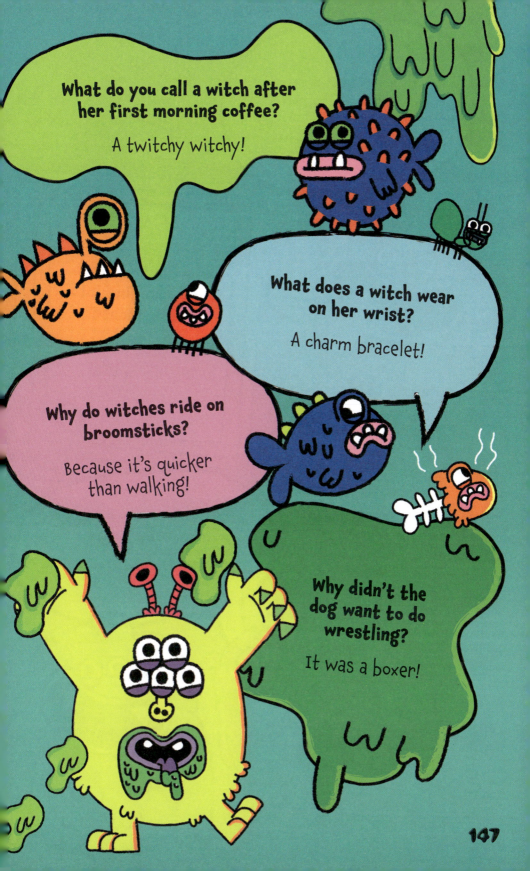

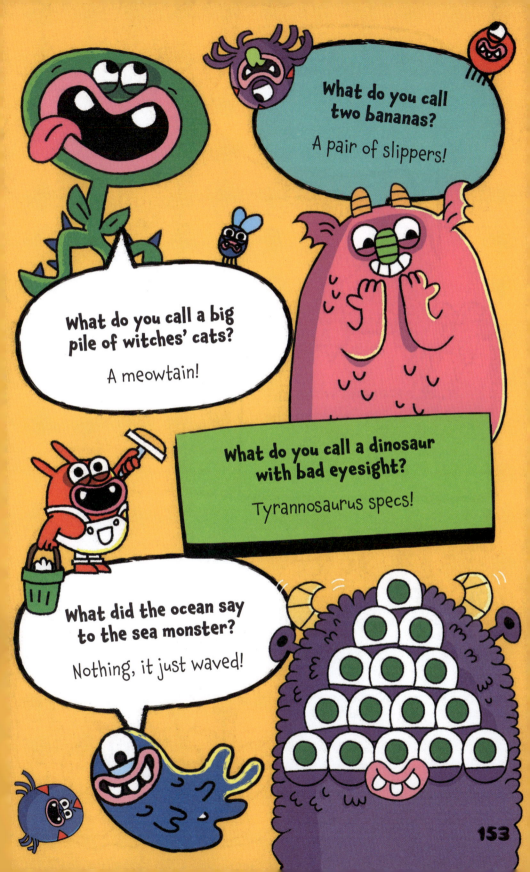

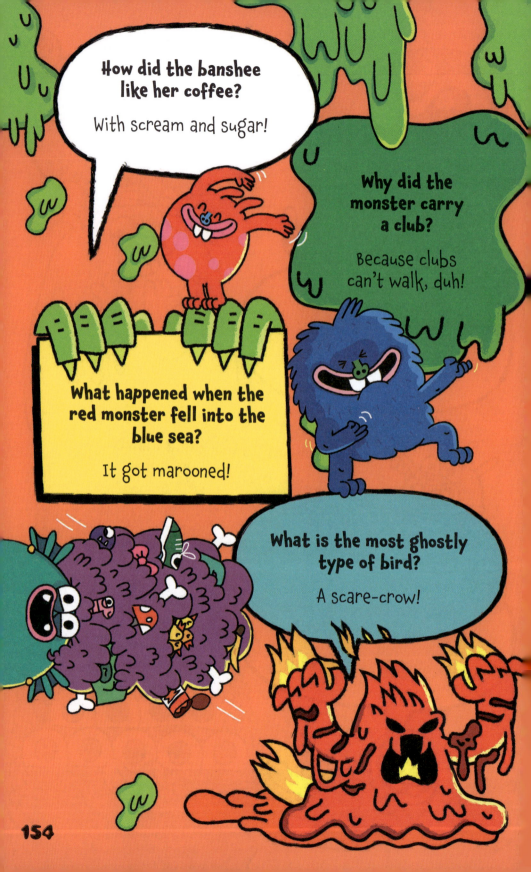

Chapter 10
Horrible Howlers